One:
LEWES
HISTORY

The enchanting town of Lewes is built on the arm of a hillside reaching down to the Ouse river valley. Surrounded by downs, marshes and farmland, it makes for an atmospheric and impressive sight from afar *(seen here from Malling Hill looking west and, inset, looking east from Offham Hill)*. There is clear evidence of pre-Roman settlement around Lewes *(see also pages 4-5)*, especially at nearby Mount Caburn, and also Roman activity itself. However, it was principally the Saxons who, around 500 AD, began the layout that developed into the town we see today. Some believe the name 'Lewes' is at least partly derived from the Old English word 'hlaewas', meaning mounds or hills.

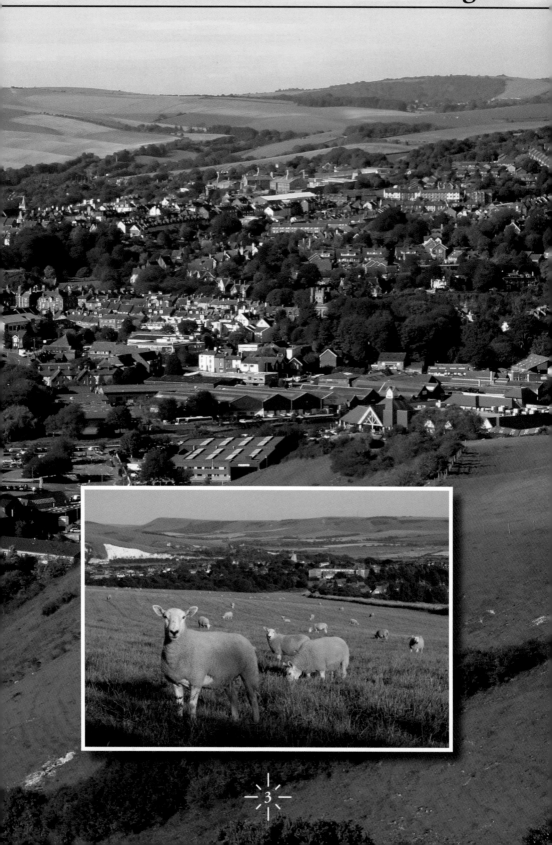

Ancient Lewes?

In recent years, there has been increased debate about the origins of the mysterious huge mounds once scattered around Lewes. Sadly, most were removed in the 18th and 19th centuries, but a fine example remains in the shape of 'The Tump' at Mountfield Road *(below)*. Although it is dismissed by some as an Elizabethan folly or slurry mound, new evidence and The Tump's curious alignments within the landscape suggest possible ritualistic pre-Roman origins, akin to Wiltshire's famous Silbury Hill.

Likewise, the huge mound on which the castle perches *(main photo)*, together with its nearby sister Brack Mount at Castle Banks *(above)*, have long been thought to be specifically constructed Norman mottes, but the discovery of ritual bones and pottery hint at earlier ancestry. Some believe Lewes was once an important complex of sacred mounds, perhaps explaining the mysterious 'feel' to some parts of the town.

The Battle of Lewes is commemorated today with the distinctive memorial helmet installed in 1965 at Lewes Priory grounds *(above and right)*. Many of Henry III's men camped at the Priory in 1264, commandeering its services on the eve of battle.

The Norman invasion of 1066 on the nearby Sussex shores of Pevensey led to a political stability of sorts within England, albeit one enforced with an iron rod *(see pages 8-9)*, but 200 years later the power of the Norman kings was being challenged and rebellion reared its head. Of all events in Lewes, the most historically significant was the battle of 1264 which took place on the hills north-west of the town between what is now Offham and Nevill *(main picture)*. Principally the climax of a dispute between the English barons, led by Simon de Montfort, against the ruling King Henry III, anger over increased taxes and royal indifference finally boiled over into violence. Aided by his loyal ally Lord John de Warrene, resident of Lewes Castle, Henry led his forces into the town on 13th May 1264 and battle was engaged the next day as de Montfort's men attacked from Offham Hill. A series of savage skirmishes left the King's men unexpectedly defeated. Tragically, over 2,700 soldiers lay dead by the end of the day (even now remains are still occasionally found in the fields), and Lewes burned as the barons advanced into the town. The King's brother fled to the safety of a windmill and Henry himself took refuge in Lewes Priory *(pages 12-13)*, from where he finally negotiated a surrender.

The settlement reached between the barons and the King ('The Mise of Lewes') was ultimately significant for the nation as a whole. As the first real legal dilution of royal powers, it indirectly paved the way for the parliamentary system we know now. Thus Lewes, which still today champions freedom of expression and liberty, played a memorable role in shaping the future of global democracy.

Standing impressively at the highest point of the town (on a mound which some argue may have been there long before the Normans arrived - *see pages 4-5*), the castle dominates Lewes. What now seems a quaint English affectation was in fact built, as most Norman castles were, as a symbol of power, reminding the invaded locals who was now in charge. The castle also served as a watchtower, with unbroken views to the south coast.

Saxon homes were ruthlessly torn down to make way for the castle complex, and Lewes was encased within walls (now gone), all planned and built by one of William the Conqueror's most loyal supporters, Earl William de Warrene (whose descendant would fight for Henry III in the later Battle of Lewes). As such, much of the enduring geography of the town centre was shaped around the vision of de Warrene, who also founded the Cluniac Priory in Southover *(see pages 12-13)*. The castle, begun soon after 1066, was constructed in stages over many years, with the towers being added in the 13th century. Beseiged during the Battle of Lewes, it saw little action thereafter. By the 1700s the castle had fallen into disuse. Restoration began in the 1800s and now it is one of Lewes' finest attractions and landmarks.

The castle gateway, one of Lewes' best-loved sights, was built in the 14th century. The Barbican Museum of local history now sits adjacent to it, where entry to the castle can be purchased.

Anne of Cleves House is a striking Tudor building in Southover High Street, given to ex-queen Anne by Henry VIII as part of his divorce settlement.

It is not known whether Anne of Cleves ever visited the house, but a later wife of a monarch-to-be certainly did, when the Duchess of Cornwall officially opened a new set of iron gates in 2006 *(right)*.

Anne of Cleves House is now an important town museum, with many fascinating exhibits.

The remains of Lewes Priory lie to the south of Priory Street in Southover and are an essential part of any historical exploration of the town.

The Priory of St Pancras was founded by William de Warrene around 1077, and after many years of development became one of the largest and most important monastries of the French Cluniac order, servicing - and taxing - the local community. Even with the impressive ruins we have today, it is almost impossible to imagine its original vastness. A mural in Friars Walk *(right)* today commemorates the work of the Priory monks.

The Priory met a dramatic end by fire and demolition, courtesy of Henry VIII's rejection of Catholicism and the Dissolution of the Monastries in 1537. Centuries later, in 1847, the graves of founder William de Warrene and his wife Gundrada were discovered nearby during railway construction.

The ivied tower near The Priory (right) is in fact a modern folly, but sits rather well with its surroundings.

13

The Lewes Martyrs

The religious chaos that followed Henry VIII's death reached its nadir between 1555 and 1557, when Queen Mary briefly reverted England to Catholicism and martyred over 300 Protestant loyalists. Seventeen of these died in Lewes during these years, burned in the streets outside what is today the Town Hall. Consequently, religious feelings ran high in Lewes for many years, as evidenced in its bonfire traditions *(pages 72-78)*.

In 1901 a memorial monument was erected on Cliffe Hill *(main photos)*, overlooking the town as a reminder of past tragedies and the human cost of tyranny.

On Bonfire Night, a banner *(above)* is now strung over Cliffe High Street, commemorating the Lewes martyrs. Thankfully, after the Marian persecutions, Lewes never saw such horrors again and the town remained miraculously unscathed during the English Civil War of the 1640s.

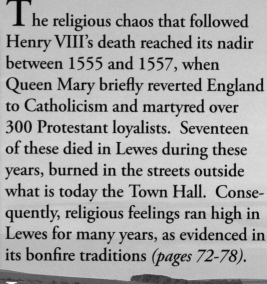

Over the centuries, many well-known figures have lived in Lewes *(see next page for one prominent example)*. Some of their homes still remain. Above can be seen the High Street house of Dr Gideon Mantell, the very first person officially to discover and identify dinosaur bones. To the right is a converted windmill in Pipe Passage that once belonged to the 'Bloomsbury Set' author Virginia Woolf in the 1930s. John Evelyn, the 17th century diarist, lived his boyhood years in Southover Grange *(see page 43)*.

Thomas Paine

Of all the famous Lewes residents, in terms of influence, one stands tall above the others: Thomas Paine. From an unlikely background in corset-manufacturing, seamanship and Customs & Excise, Paine became one of the most prominent political radicals of the 18th century. His writings and campaigning for the 'rights of man' - always speaking out for the underdog - led to his direct influence in both the War for American Independence and the French Revolution. It can't be denied that Paine made as many enemies as friends, but his political legacy lives on today and he serves as an example to all of someone fearlessly taking a stand in the face of oppression.

This beautiful mural by Julian Bell commemorates Thomas Paine and is situated beneath the Market Tower in Market Street (see page 32).

'A long habit of not thinking a thing wrong gives it a superficial appearance of being right'
- THOMAS PAINE

Thomas Paine resided in Lewes between 1768 and 1774, living at Bull House *(below)* in the High Street, where he met and married - albeit briefly - his land-lord's daughter Elizabeth. Many evenings were spent arguing with friends over politics and ideals at the nearby White Hart Inn, which remains there now *(right)*. These gatherings were formally known as the 'Headstrong Club', a modern version of which still thrives. Paine's life ended in relative obscurity in America but, even near the end, he still wrote of his formative days in Lewes.

The Lewes Avalanche

Lewes sounds like the unlikeliest place for an avalanche but, on 27th December 1848, precisely such an event occurred from the cliffs above what is now South Street, after an unusually large fall of snow. Eight residents died when their homes were crushed.

The site of the 1848 avalanche is occupied today by The Snowdrop pub - a deceptively pretty name that commemorates the event.

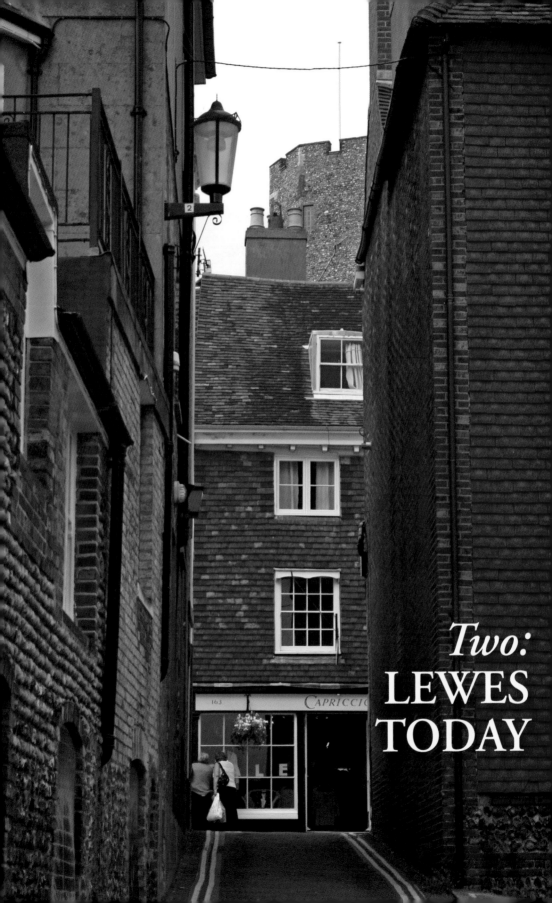

Two:
LEWES
TODAY

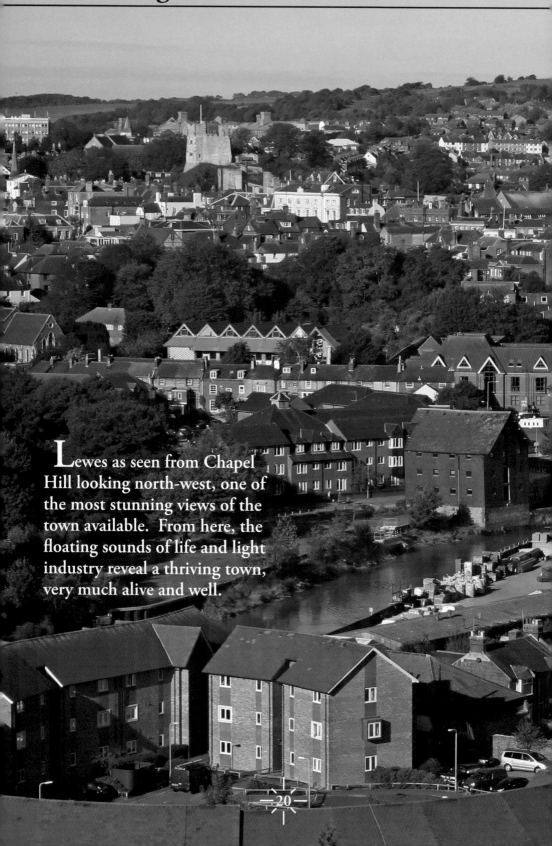

Lewes as seen from Chapel Hill looking north-west, one of the most stunning views of the town available. From here, the floating sounds of life and light industry reveal a thriving town, very much alive and well.

The High Street

The western part of the High Street (before School Hill sweeps down towards Cliffe), a diverse mix of architectural styles.

Looking east down School Hill towards Cliffe, the golden evening light illuminates the elevated estate of Cuilfail and the needle of the Martyrs' Memorial.

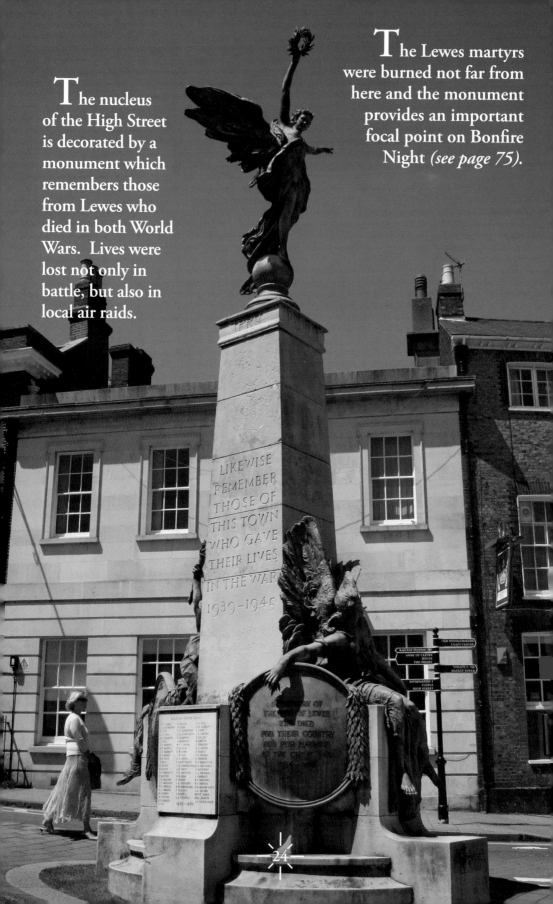

The nucleus of the High Street is decorated by a monument which remembers those from Lewes who died in both World Wars. Lives were lost not only in battle, but also in local air raids.

The Lewes martyrs were burned not far from here and the monument provides an important focal point on Bonfire Night *(see page 75).*

LIKEWISE REMEMBER THOSE OF THIS TOWN WHO GAVE THEIR LIVES IN THE WAR 1939-1945

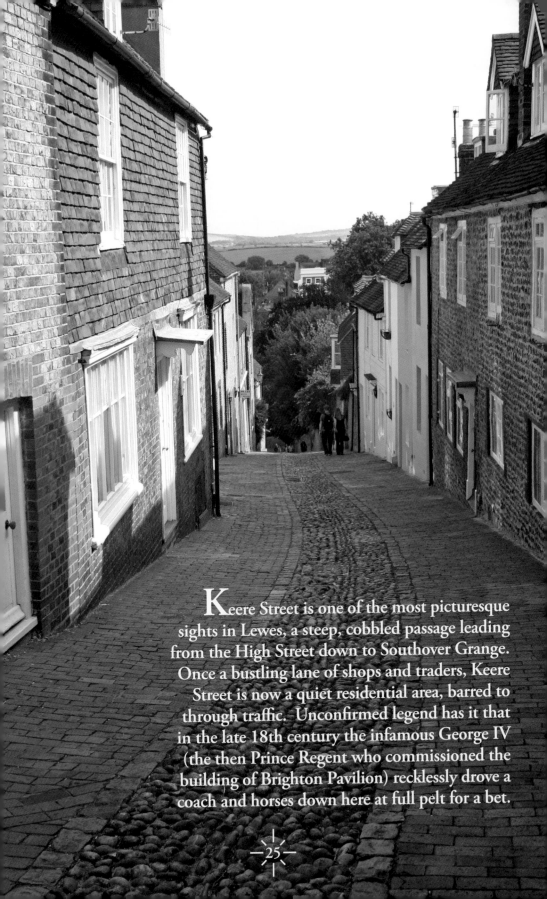

Keere Street is one of the most picturesque sights in Lewes, a steep, cobbled passage leading from the High Street down to Southover Grange. Once a bustling lane of shops and traders, Keere Street is now a quiet residential area, barred to through traffic. Unconfirmed legend has it that in the late 18th century the infamous George IV (the then Prince Regent who commissioned the building of Brighton Pavilion) recklessly drove a coach and horses down here at full pelt for a bet.

Lewes is criss-crossed by a series of narrow passageways known locally as 'twittens' (probably derived from the words 'betwixt and between'). The main layout of the twittens dates back to Norman times, when the town was reconstructed around the new castle and largely contained within strong encircling walls. Only fragments of the old town walls now remain.

Some twittens, like Pipe Passage *(opposite top)*, follow the path of the town walls, but the majority simply pass from north to south, connecting the higher ground of the High Street with the lower roads to the south, as with the finest example at Church Twitten *(above)*. Other passageways *(like the residential one which leads off Malling Street, opposite below)*, though newer, share a similar style.

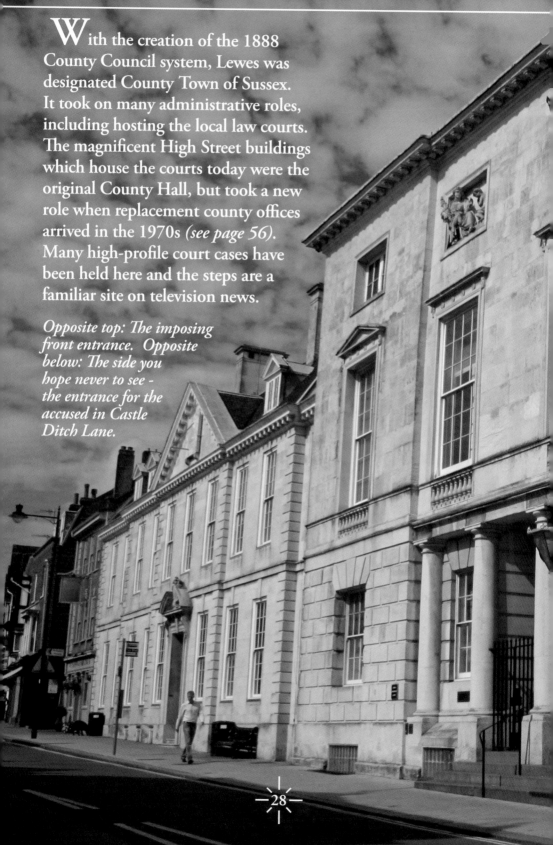

The Law Courts

With the creation of the 1888 County Council system, Lewes was designated County Town of Sussex. It took on many administrative roles, including hosting the local law courts. The magnificent High Street buildings which house the courts today were the original County Hall, but took a new role when replacement county offices arrived in the 1970s *(see page 56)*. Many high-profile court cases have been held here and the steps are a familiar site on television news.

Opposite top: The imposing front entrance. Opposite below: The side you hope never to see - the entrance for the accused in Castle Ditch Lane.

The impressive Town Hall we see today was opened in 1893, replacing the old version built in the 1700s (which stood as a separate tower in the High Street). The Town Hall forms part of the same complex as the huge Corn Exchange, housing civic offices and providing an important communal space for shows, functions and exhibitions. Rodin's famous sculpture 'The Kiss' was even displayed here in 1999 - a brief homecoming for the artwork, which was stored away in Lewes for years in the early 20th century before its worth was realised.

Visitors should remember to look upwards while strolling the streets of Lewes. The town is home to several fascinating and attractive clock towers and spires.

MARKET St

The Market Tower, not far from the War Memorial, was built in 1791, providing a market space beneath and housing 'Gabriel' - the official town bell. Today, its internal upper rooms serve as the headquarters for the Lewes Operatic Society, which has been impressively active since 1911.

The official town clock *(above left)* hangs over the High Street from the hall of St Michael's Church *(see page 52)*. It is a memorable sight, if rather prone to costly breakdowns. A rather more Gothic clock tower can be found atop Fitzroy House *(main photo)* in Friars Walk.

Georgian times produced many architectural styles, including the development of 'mathematical tiles' - small facing-tiles which cover outer walls and emulate brick-work, thus enabling timber-framed houses or basic brick constructions to take on a more elegant and substantial appearance. Lewes is famed for its many excellent 18th century examples, although discerning brick from tile is not always an easy task.

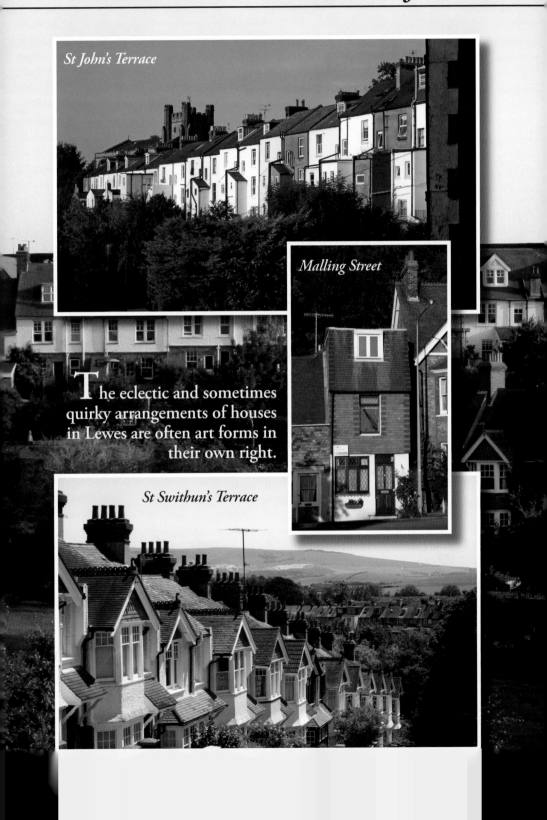

St John's Terrace

Malling Street

The eclectic and sometimes quirky arrangements of houses in Lewes are often art forms in their own right.

St Swithun's Terrace

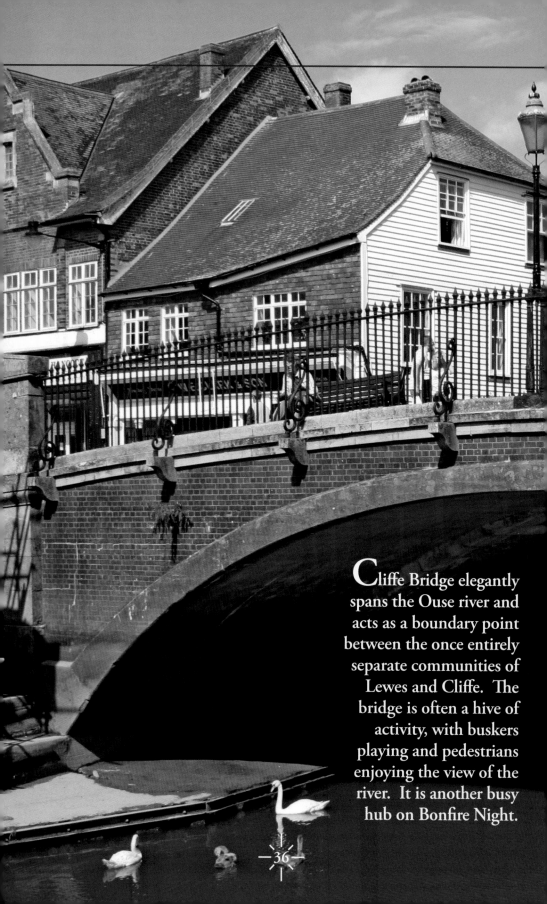

Cliffe Bridge elegantly spans the Ouse river and acts as a boundary point between the once entirely separate communities of Lewes and Cliffe. The bridge is often a hive of activity, with buskers playing and pedestrians enjoying the view of the river. It is another busy hub on Bonfire Night.

Cliffe Bridge

The bridge we see today (which itself replaced earlier wooden versions) was first built in 1727 and has undergone many changes since then to accommodate increased usage and the advent of the car. The opening of the Phoenix Causeway relief bridge in 1969 and the more recent pedestrianisation of Cliffe has eased its stresses.

Cliffe

Cliffe and South Street comprise the easternmost areas of the old town, a mix of the industrial *(see page 40)* and the quaint, as with the entrance to Chapel Hill *(below)*.

That residents of Cliffe still fiercely defend a spirit of independence, especially on Bonfire Night *(see pages 72-73)*, is a hangover from the centuries when Cliffe was a separate settlement east of the river, below the chalk cliffs that give the district its name. The Ouse was once crucial to the industrial lifeblood of the town, and the now converted warehouses *(main photo)* to the south of Cliffe Bridge are a slightly poignant reminder of a time when Lewes was a thriving port. Surprisingly large ships and barges would sail up the Ouse from the sea at Newhaven. The rise of road haulage and the decline of southern industry in the 20th century would change this irrevocably, but Cliffe still retains a sense of vitality. Its unique atmosphere can be felt all day, but strolling along Cliffe High Street in quiet moments of summer evening sunshine *(below)* has a special magic.

Harvey's Brewery

Glowing in the setting sun, the most cherished industry of Lewes - Harvey's Brewery - was established in 1790 and sits on the eastern banks of the Ouse between Cliffe Bridge and the Phoenix Causeway. Its presence is felt most when the delightfully heady scent of malted hops fills the air.

Providing beer for many Sussex pubs (and beyond), the brewery's independence and influence, like Cliffe itself, are fiercely defended by ale aficionados and protectors of local produce in the face of steely competition from outside 'big business'.

Cuilfail and Chapel Hill

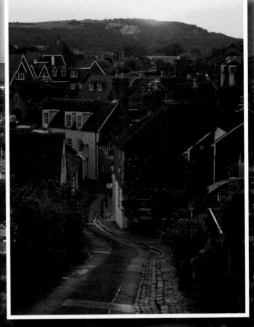

The opening of the Cuilfail relief tunnel in 1979, with its charming ammonite entrance monument *(above left)*, transformed previously traffic-bound Cliffe and Chapel Hill *(main photos)* into quieter places.

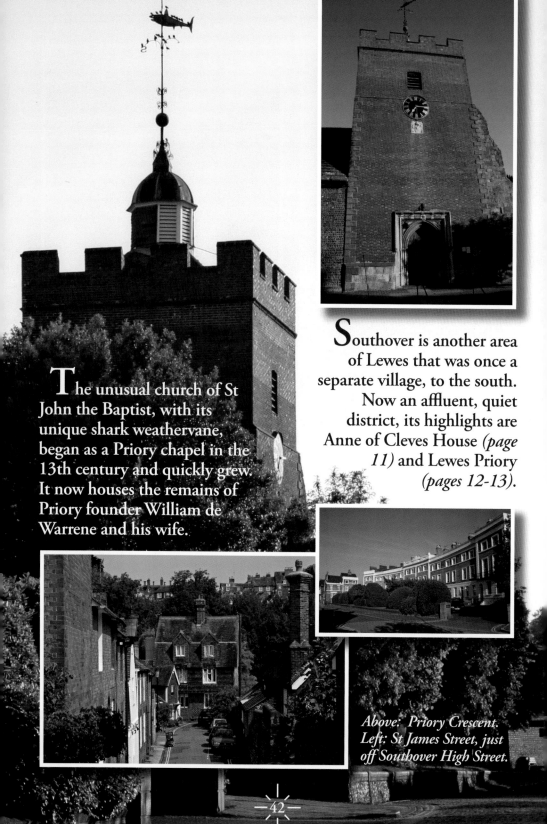

The unusual church of St John the Baptist, with its unique shark weathervane, began as a Priory chapel in the 13th century and quickly grew. It now houses the remains of Priory founder William de Warrene and his wife.

Southover is another area of Lewes that was once a separate village, to the south. Now an affluent, quiet district, its highlights are Anne of Cleves House *(page 11)* and Lewes Priory *(pages 12-13).*

Above: Priory Crescent.
Left: St James Street, just off Southover High Street.

Southover Grange and its public garden is arguably the most attractive relaxation spot in Lewes. Built in 1572 with stones from the dismantled Priory, the Grange itself today houses the Registry Office.

On warm sunny days, The Grange, with its tea hatch, benches and lawns, is a safe, happy place for people to lounge and children to play.

Nevill, Landport and Malling

Three of the major housing estates of Lewes can be seen in this photo: Nevill *(far top left)*, Landport *(middle)*, and parts of Malling *(foreground and to the right)*. Malling fills the valley to the north-east of Lewes, while Landport and Nevill climb the gentler slopes of the downs on which Saxon Lewes was developed.

A large proportion of Lewes' population lives in these estates, but of the three only Malling really has room to grow (perhaps thankfully, from an environmental viewpoint), as the enclosed landscape around Lewes places natural limits on its expansion.

Around the Districts

Lewes' charm extends beyond its centre, and beauty can be found afield in all sorts of architecture and pleasing topography: Mount Pleasant, with the Elephant & Castle pub on the left *(top left)*; Bell Lane, leading to the Winterbourne Estate *(below left)*; Leicester Road *(opposite top right)*; flats at Abergavenny Road *(opposite below right)*.

Public Houses

The Lewes Arms pub in Mount Place (left), one of the best-loved local alehouses, found itself in a storm of national publicity when local brew Harvey's was dropped from its pumps in 2006. A customer boycott and a highly-publicised protest campaign ensured the beer's eventual return (above).

Lewes is home to many varied and attractive pubs in the old-fashioned non-corporate tradition, of which these are just a few: The Swan in Southover High Street *(opposite below)*; The King's Head in Priory Street *(above)*; The Black Horse in Western Road *(right)*. There were once double the number of public houses in Lewes - one on almost every corner! *(See page 53 for the remains of a lost one.)*

Above: *The Friends Meeting House, Friar's Walk. Quakers have had a strong presence in Lewes since their founding in the 1600s.* Below: *The Anglican St John sub Castro, Lancaster Street (on the site of some of the removed mounds - see page 4).* Main background: *The Catholic St Pancras, Irelands Lane.*

Christianity has always had a strong influence in Lewes, but the denominations are many and varied, with 'non-con-formist' religions particularly active. Whatever one's view of the beliefs, the churches of Lewes are artworks in themselves: The Presbyterian Jireh Chapel *(above)*, recently restored, is a unique local example of such architecture. The Anglican St Thomas à Becket in Cliffe *(right)* is more traditional.

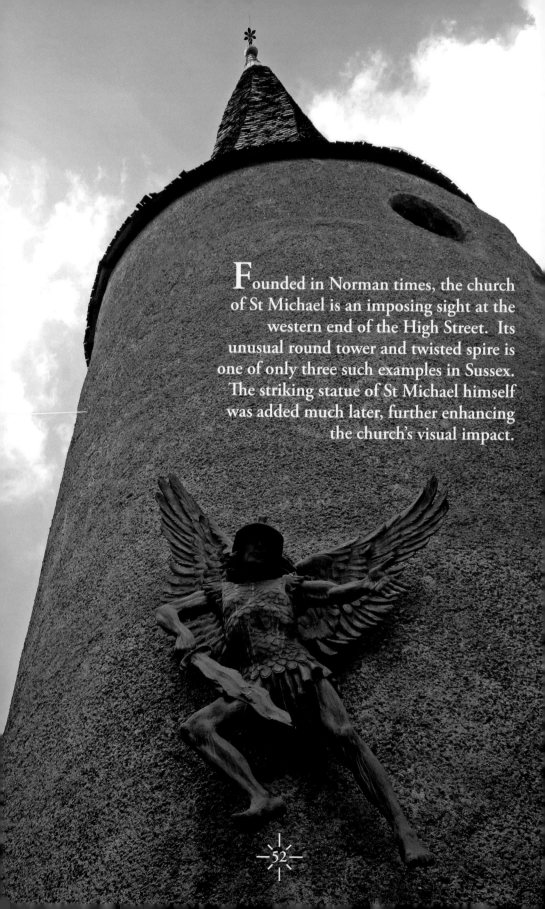

Founded in Norman times, the church of St Michael is an imposing sight at the western end of the High Street. Its unusual round tower and twisted spire is one of only three such examples in Sussex. The striking statue of St Michael himself was added much later, further enhancing the church's visual impact.

Lewes is full of mysterious little monuments: The White Lion (right) *in Westgate Street is the old sign from a now demolished pub;* the disused 1874 drinking fountain (below right) *makes for a rustic sight in Friars Walk;* the pavement plaque in Western Road (below left) *marks the spot where the famous Greenwich Meridian Line passes through Lewes - the town sits at zero degrees longitude!*

The importance of the Ouse river to the development of Lewes is often overlooked. Its presence shaped the topography of the land and thus the town itself and the way many of its districts grew. The access the Ouse gave to shipping in earlier centuries was a vital lifeline in Lewes' growth as a thriving centre of industry and influence; today, river traffic has dwindled to the occasional pleasure boat. Decades of silting now prevent large vessels entering, so the Ouse's modern appeal is primarily scenic, as demonstrated in views from Landport *(opposite top)*, South Street *(opposite below)* and Offham Hill *(main photo)*. The river is not always a friend, though. In 1960 and 2000, floods devastated the town, and debates about new defences rage on.

Another Side to Lewes

All the postcard scenery can make one forget that there is a less glamorous side to the administrative functions of Lewes. County Hall *(left)*, built in 1969, looking deceivingly fair in the morning sun, is regularly described as 'The Most Hated Building in Lewes', dominating the skyline from many viewpoints with its hard and unimaginative 1960s angles. Curiously, it seems to be more loathed than the other grimly domineering structure at the western end of town; Lewes Prison *(below)*, one of Britain's busiest gaols.

Three:
LEWES
LIFE

HARVEYS

HARVEY & SON   BREWERS   LEWES

FOUNDED 1790

HARVEYS

A Market Town

As years have gone by, the livestock auctions and street markets that used to define daily life in Lewes have, as with most towns today, retreated in the wake of superstores and franchises. But Lewes' market spirit still flourishes on occasion, such as at the monthly farmers' markets in the Town Square *(main photo).*

Some shops, as with Beckworths High Street deli seen here, still retain a market-like atmosphere.

Another market-like event is the weekly Boot Fair, held in Eastgate car park (above). For some, the Sunday morning stroll for bargains and bric-a-brac becomes a cherished ritual.

WH
S

A busy cafe culture thrives in Lewes, with Bill's *(this page)* and the Riverside Centre *(opposite)* being two of the most popular spots.

Bill's began as a fresh produce store, with an air of the greengrocers of old, but the development of its cafe, with its bustling and friendly air, has made it a key part of Cliffe's growing role as the central heart of Lewes.

The Riverside Centre *(this page)*, converted from the old motor garage that stood in Cliffe for many years, has become another favourite haunt for locals and visitors. Its attractive and compact mix of cafes, shops and stalls just off the main Town Square (across which the Uckfield to Lewes railway once arched ominously) has helped the area's successful ongoing regeneration.

Distinctive Shops

Left: The proprietor of Catlin's shares the aroma of his wares.

One of the appeals of Lewes is its diverse mix of independent shops, still surviving despite the encroachment of chain stores and charity outlets. Catlin's, in the upper High Street *(above and right)*, for example, is one of just a few tobacconists left in Sussex and has operated continuously (with only name changes) since 1915.

Left: Bonne Bouche, a little chocolate shop sweetly tucked away in St Martin's Lane, just off the High Street.

Some more distinctive shops of Lewes: May's organic goods store has been a bonus to Cliffe (right); Filler's sandwich bar in Market Street (centre right) is a busy lunch spot.

King's Framers in the High Street (above) always offers attractive window displays, as does Cliffe High Street interior furnisher Simon David (right).

The Fifteenth Century Book-shop at the top of Keere Street *(see page 25)* is one of the finest remaining examples of unspoilt Tudor architecture in Lewes, its beams authentically daubed.

The Needlemakers in West Street is a complex of craft shops and grotto-like 'collectable' emporiums. A wishing well and cafe adds to its appeal.

Utilising the infra-structure of disused surgical needle and candle factories, The Needlemakers was saved from demolition to become a valuable addition to Lewes.

Leisure Time

Leisure pursuits in Lewes are many and varied. Its facilities provide for all interests and include a local football club (Lewes FC) and adjoining cricket fields *(background photo)*.

Top: Children play in the popular gardens of Southover Grange (see page 43).

Middle: Bowls are played in what was once the old 'tilting' (jousting) ground of the castle.

Bottom: The sedate martial art of T'ai Chi at The Priory fields.

Top: A television drama being filmed on Cliffe Bridge.

Middle: Fishing at The Pells - narrow lakes by Pelham Terrace. A cherished outdoor swimming pool lies nearby.

Bottom: Morris dancing, a popular local pastime, at the John Harvey Tavern, Bear Lane.

Aside from Bonfire Night *(see pages 72-78)*, Lewes hosts many other active annual events, particularly during summer, including a guitar festival, a carnival, and, seen here, a children's parade, organised by leaving-age years of local schools.

Lewes is home to one of southern England's longest running amateur pantomimes, presented each January at the hall of St Mary's Social Centre. This anarchic and fun event has been staged for over 60 years.

F amiliar places to Lewes residents...

Top: Lewes Library, just off Friar's Walk.

Below: The railway station in, naturally, Station Road.

Below: The All Saints Centre, a converted church in Friars Walk, now a crucial Lewes venue for films, music, classes and lectures, as seen lower right with an event organised by the Lewes-based Changing Times group.

Four:
LEWES IN
WINTER

Bonfire Night

As summer fades into autumn, the town prepares for the biggest night of its annual calendar.

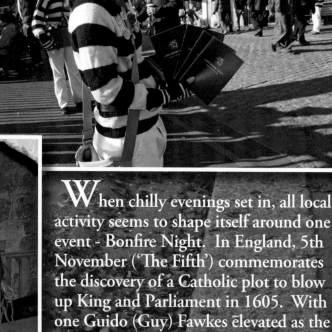

Guido Fawkes Traitor

When chilly evenings set in, all local activity seems to shape itself around one event - Bonfire Night. In England, 5th November ('The Fifth') commemorates the discovery of a Catholic plot to blow up King and Parliament in 1605. With one Guido (Guy) Fawkes elevated as the chief villain of the 'Gunpowder Plot', it was decreed that the day of deliverance be forever marked. Lewes, perhaps with memories of its Protestant martyrs *(see page 14)*, has never forgotten this decree.

Banners hang over Cliffe High Street on the morning of 5th November, while nervous shopkeepers begin to board up their windows (opposite and this page background) to protect themselves from the riskier side of the festivities.

IN MEMORY OF

DIRICK CARVER
THOMAS HARLAND
JOHN OSWALD
THOMAS AVINGTON
THOMAS REED
THOMAS WOOD
THOMAS MYLES
RICHARD WOODMAN
GEORGE STEVENS

ALEXANDER HOSMAN
WILLIAM MAINARD
THOMAS A NEWOOD
MARGERY MORRIS
JAMES MORRIS
DENIS BURGES
ANN ASHDON
MARY GROVES

PROTESTANT MARTYRS OF LEWES
1555 - 1557
"FAITHFUL UNTO DEATH"

There are five major bonfire societies, though Cliffe perhaps makes its presence felt more than most, hanging its controversial 'No Popery' banners across Cliffe High Street to annual local - and sometimes national - debate.

While Bonfire festivities have faded in other parts of the country, Lewes has steadfastly held to its traditions. Bonfire Societies hold fund-raising events throughout the year and emerge in the weeks before The Fifth selling programmes (this page and opposite) in their smuggler-like costumes. When red paper fragments from Chinese crackers appear in the gutter (opposite background), Bonfire Night is near.

Seventeen burning crosses commemorate the Lewes martyrs - and make their wider point.

On Bonfire Night itself, the societies parade their territorial areas of the town with flaming torches to the sound of marching bands and

One of the most poignant and moving rituals of The Fifth is the remembrance of the 'glorious dead' at the War Memorial, showing respect to those who fell in both World Wars and other conflicts. 'The Last Post' is played by each society in turn and firework poppies are lit. The area around the memorial is crammed for this, the most solemn part of the evening, before the atmosphere lightens and more disrespectful fun begins.

Freedom of Expression

For a town sometimes perceived as genteel on its surface, on just one night of the year Lewes erupts into a cry of defiance against tyranny and injustice. On 5th November (or 4th, if Bonfire Night falls on a Sunday) effigies of Guy Fawkes, politicians, local trouble-makers or errant celebrities are paraded through the streets before being blown up at one of the five major bonfire sites. Marchers revel in the joy of having the freedom of the streets, albeit temporarily. The entire town is shut off and cars are banned.

Nervous police patrol the streets, seemingly uneasy at the sponsored anarchy before them, and marchers and the thousands upon thousands of visitors who flood into town for the spectacle (despite the pleas of the organisers to leave Lewes to itself on the night) delight at the brief liberation from society's usual shackles.

This page and opposite top: Commercial Square gathers for 'bonfire prayers' and delightfully non-PC sermons at its head-quarters in Mount Place.

Each main society - Borough, Cliffe, Commercial Square, South Street and Waterloo - have their own individual traditions and territories, operating from different headquarters around the town on the night, to where they eventually retire after their spectacular firework displays for 'bonfire prayers' and drink-aided revelries. Cliffe is strongest on its religious traditions, and although there is no animosity towards Catholics today, it still insists on parading an effigy of the 17th century Pope Paul V through the streets *(below)* and exploding another later.

The papal effigy and banners create friction and debate each year, but societies fear the erosion of tradition will destroy the essence of free speech that Bonfire Night embodies.

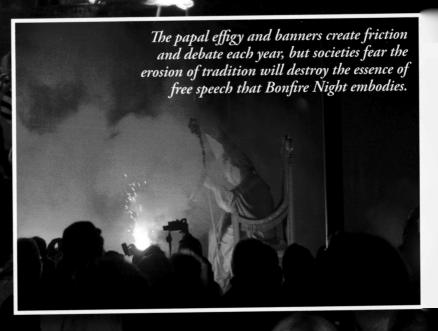

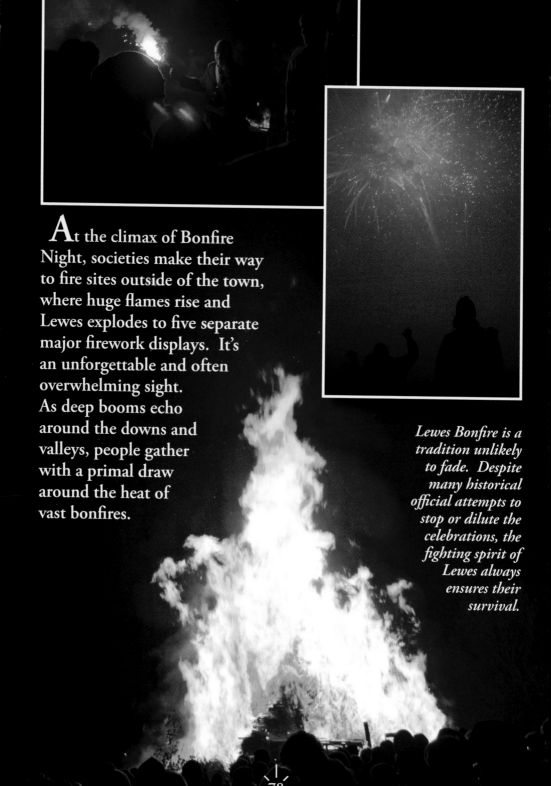

At the climax of Bonfire Night, societies make their way to fire sites outside of the town, where huge flames rise and Lewes explodes to five separate major firework displays. It's an unforgettable and often overwhelming sight. As deep booms echo around the downs and valleys, people gather with a primal draw around the heat of vast bonfires.

Lewes Bonfire is a tradition unlikely to fade. Despite many historical official attempts to stop or dilute the celebrations, the fighting spirit of Lewes always ensures their survival.

And after the fire,.. comes the ice. As Bonfire recedes into an autumn memory for another year and winter takes hold, Lewes can sometimes take on a completely new demeanour.

Winter Transformation

In these days of apparent climate change, snow is rarer in Lewes than it once was, but when it comes, the wait is worthwhile.

This page: Southover Grange makes for a stunning sight when snow arrives, and children soon leave their mark.

Opposite top left: Steam rises evocatively from Harvey's Brewery in the cold winter air.

Opposite top right: Snowy gates at Castle Precinct.

Opposite below: White rooftops at Cliffe, as seen from Chapel Hill.

Background: The Avenue.

Above: Almost a Christmas card view of The Grange walls from Southover High Street.

Left: Snowy wastes looking towards Firle from the top of Lewes Golf Club.

Below: A snowman in the making at The Grange.

The horizon brightens looking towards Newhaven from Lewes Golf Club, with the Ouse snaking its way out towards the sea. With the passing of winter, Lewes looks forward once again to warmer months and longer evenings of colour and light.

Epilogue

*The Sun sinks gloriously over
Lewes, as seen from Chapel Hill.*

Lewes, apparently serene and
ordered on the surface, is a town
of great complexity and resolve,
always fighting for the freedom to
speak out loud and be itself. Many
of its inhabitants, past and present,
have embodied this quality with
a passion for the place that goes
beyond an appreciation of beauty.
Long may that passion live